ALTERNATOR BOOKS™

UNEXPLAINED

THE POLTERGEIST ENIGMA

Craig Boutland

Lerner Publications ◆ Minneapolis

Lerner Publications Company
A division of Lerner Publishing Group, Inc.
241 First Avenue North
Minneapolis, MN 55401 USA

For reading levels and more information, look up this title at www.lernerbooks.com.

Main body text set in Minion Pro.
Font provided by Adobe Systems.

Library of Congress Cataloging-in-Publication Data

Names: Boutland, Craig, author.
Title: The poltergeist enigma / Craig Boutland.
Description: Minneapolis : Lerner Publications, [2019] | Series: Unexplained (alternator books) | Audience: Age: 8–12. | Audience: Grade: 4–6. | Includes bibliographical references and index.
Identifiers: LCCN 2019001063 (print) | LCCN 2019003931 (ebook) | ISBN 9781541562905 (eb pdf) | ISBN 9781541562851 (lb : alk. paper) | ISBN 9781541573796 (pb : alk. paper)
Subjects: LCSH: Poltergeists—Juvenile literature.
Classification: LCC BF1483 (ebook) | LCC BF1483 .B68 2019 (print) | DDC 133.1/42—dc23

LC record available at https://lccn.loc.gov/2019001063

Manufactured in the United States of America
1-46411-47501-4/5/2019

Contents

Introduction

Poltergeists are angry spirits. The word poltergeist comes from the German word *poltern*, which means to make a noise, and *geist*, or ghost. People who are visited by poltergeists say they make noises, such as rapping or banging. Sometimes, the spirit laughs or even speaks. It often speaks in more than one language.

Moving Things Around

Poltergeists also move things. They throw things at people. Sometimes they break things. They even create fires or puddles of water. There are often young people in the houses where poltergeists have appeared. Some experts think they cause poltergeists to appear. Could this possibly be true?

Poltergeists in History

In many countries there are stories about spirits that enjoy making things difficult for people. They break things, make milk go sour, and play tricks on people. These spirits are sometimes called goblins. In Norway they are called trolls. Some researchers believe these beings are actually poltergeists.

One of the first reports of a poltergeist was in Germany in the Middle Ages (about 500-1500). A German farmer and his family were attacked in 858 in a place called Bingen. The poltergeist threw stones at the family. It pounded on the walls of their farmhouse and burned the crops. The farmer asked his local priests to **exorcize** the poltergeist, but the poltergeist threw stones at the holy men. The record doesn't say what happened after that. Similar stories about poltergeists continued to appear in Germany.

Martin Luther

In the sixteenth century, Martin Luther, the German founder of **Protestantism**, felt he was being attacked by poltergeists. Luther believed strongly in evil and the devil. From a young age he thought that mischievous spirits were attacking him. Luther suffered from mood swings and depression throughout his life. He blamed demons for his health problems.

On October 31, 1517, Luther famously published his *Ninety-Five Theses*, which was a list of things he wanted to change in the Roman Catholic Church.

Luther stayed at Wartburg Castle while he worked on arguments to support his religious beliefs.

In his later life he said a poltergeist had visited him in his kitchen, hitting him with walnuts and smashing plates. Luther argued with many religious leaders about poltergeists. They did not believe such ghosts existed. Was Luther just imagining some of the things that had happened to him? Could his own mind have been creating the poltergeists?

Full of Energy and Anger

Electrical energy seems to have a part to play in stories about poltergeists. A poltergeist visited the Pain family in the city of Bristol, England, during the seventeenth century. The spirit made the house light up at night without using candles or electricity. The spirit also made loud banging noises.

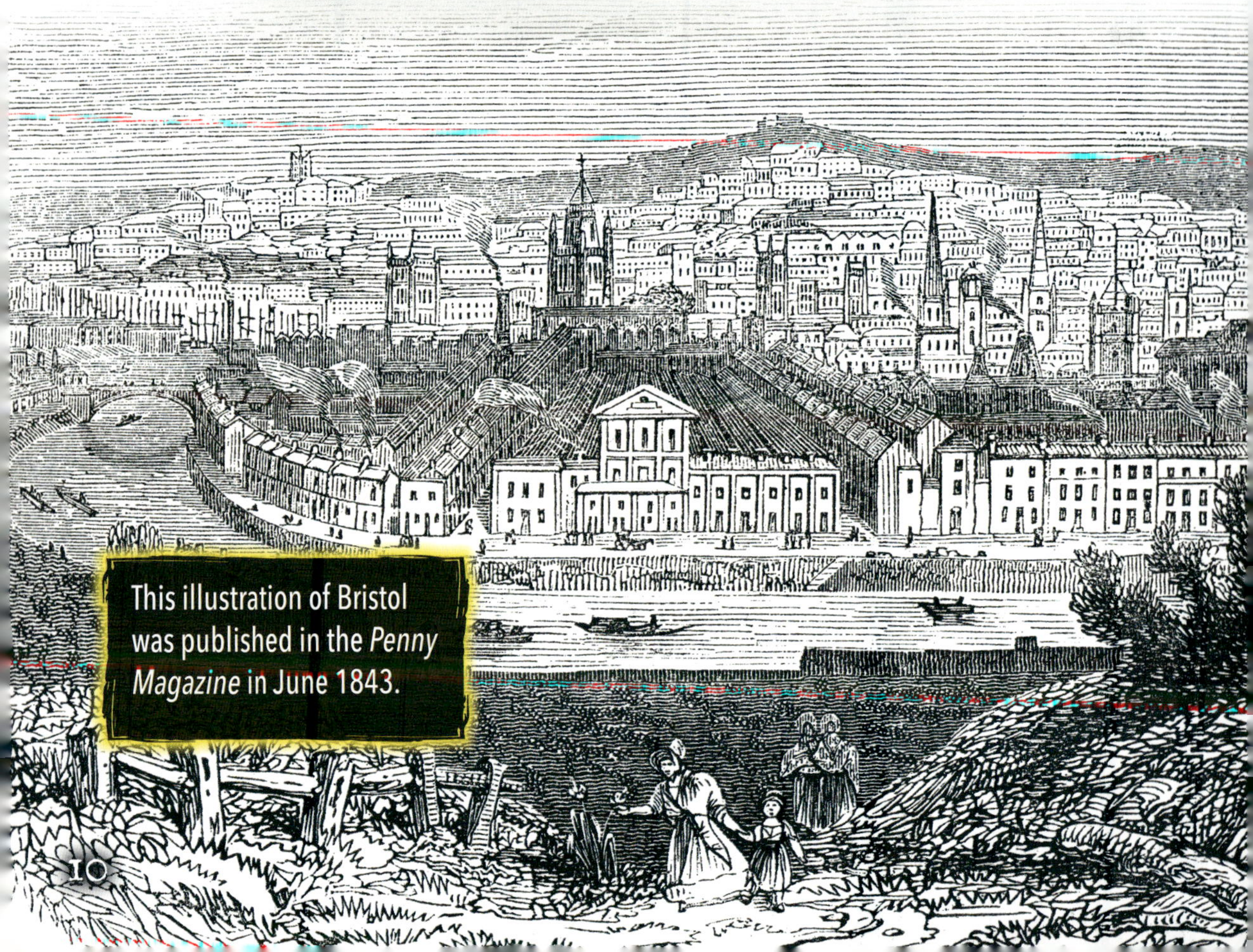

This illustration of Bristol was published in the *Penny Magazine* in June 1843.

At one point, the Pain family and a priest they had asked to help them were trapped in a room. The poltergeist had moved a heavy trunk against the door so it could not be opened. One day, the Bristol poltergeist suddenly disappeared. The family was not bothered by it again. But they had no idea why the spirit had come to visit in the first place.

The Great Amherst Mystery

In 1878, a famous and disturbing story hit the headlines in Amherst, Canada. Esther Cox was a young woman living with her family. One day a spirit arrived in the house. There were strange rustlings and bangings in the night in the room Esther shared with her sister. Blankets and pillows flew off the bed.

The cottage in Nova Scotia where Esther Cox and her family lived. People traveled specially to see the famous house.

Objects flew through the air and words appeared on the wall above Esther's bed. She began to suffer from **seizures**. A doctor was called. He saw the writing on the wall and heard the loud banging. Other witnesses also heard strange sounds and saw objects move. When Esther became ill with **diphtheria**, the visitations stopped, but they started up again as soon as she was well.

No Escape

Esther decided to move away from her home in hopes of leaving the poltergeist behind. She went to live with another nearby family. However, the spirit followed her. A ghost researcher, Walter Hubbell, visited Esther and stayed with her for six weeks. He believed her stories. In 1888 he published a book that contained statements from thirteen other witnesses who said they had seen **paranormal** activity happening around Esther.

Was Esther Cox really haunted by poltergeists?

There is no doubt that something was happening to Esther. Her body swelled up and she felt pain. There were many witnesses who saw household objects move when Esther was nowhere near them. It was clear that she was not trying to trick Hubbell and his fellow researchers.

Hubbell organized a tour of North America for Esther so she could tell her story. However, some people were hostile toward her, and she returned to Amherst. She was accused of **arson** after a barn in town burned down. She went to prison for one month, and when she returned the spirits seemed to have gone. Some people said Esther had been tricking them all along, and there were never any poltergeists.

Some people believe it is possible to bend objects such as metal spoons using the power of the mind.

All in the Mind?

The case of Esther Cox raised many questions about poltergeists. Was Esther the cause of these strange happenings? Was there some energy that came from her own mind that made objects move? Some paranormal researchers believe this is possible. They call this ability **telekinesis**.

Gef the Talking Mongoose

In the 1930s the Irving family began to hear rustling and other noises in their farmhouse on the Isle of Man, just off the coast of northwestern England. These sounds seemed to come from within the walls. Thinking the sounds were caused by rats, James Irving put out poison.

Spirit from India?

The poison had no effect. The noises continued. One night, the farmer shouted at the walls in frustration. Whatever was making the sounds listened to James and made sounds back. The farmer's thirteen-year-old daughter, Voirrey, sang nursery rhymes to it. Eventually, the creature talked back. It said it was a ghost trapped in the body of a **mongoose**. The ghost said it was named Gef.

James and Margaret Irving outside their farmhouse on the Isle of Man. Were they telling the truth about Gef the talking mongoose?

An Unusual Story

A paranormal researcher visited the Irvings and was shouted at by a high-pitched voice. He was told it was Gef, who wanted to know who the man was. Gef often hid behind hedges and made comments about people who were walking by. The family left food out for him. They said he would tell them when dangerous animals were near the farmhouse.

Scientific Research

Researchers took hairs found in the farmhouse to a laboratory. The hairs were from a dog, not a mongoose. Some paw prints were also analyzed. Some people said the hair and paw prints came from the family sheepdog. But the Irvings insisted they were from Gef, their talking mongoose.

Hairs sent to a research laboratory in 1932 were examined under a microscope.

In 1935, another paranormal researcher named Harry Price visited the farm. The farmhouse had walls covered with wooden panels. There were small gaps between these panels. Price said the walls could **amplify** sound. He said that if someone spoke into one of the many gaps in the panels, the sound would carry to different parts of the house.

The local press claimed that the haunting at the Irving farmhouse was a hoax.

Voirrey Irving was accused of creating the voice of Gef.

Newspapers reported the story of Gef. Some people claimed to have seen the mongoose. But many people said Gef was just an imaginary friend invented by Voirrey. They said she was making the noises through the walls. A journalist said that he had heard Voirrey making noises. James Irving said the journalist was mistaken. Voirrey never admitted that she was the voice of the mongoose. She died in 2005, so no one will ever know the truth.

Forces of Nature?

Poltergeists are not like other ghosts. Most ghosts are silent and do not notice humans around them. Poltergeists want to be noticed. They want to make people feel uncomfortable, and they want to change the lives of the people they are haunting.

Researchers in Rosenheim made a video of poltergeist activity. This is a frame from the video, showing a light fixture swinging from side to side.

Many researchers believe that poltergeists are fueled by energy. One poltergeist invaded a law office in Rosenheim, Bavaria, in 1967. It affected the electricity in the building. The poltergeist turned the lights on and off and interfered with the phone system. It caused lamps to swing and copy machines to break down.

Electrical Disturbance

The Rosenheim poltergeist even made **fluorescent light tubes** explode. The power company checked all the electrical circuits. The phone company checked all the phones. They could not find anything wrong. But dangerous energy was coming from somewhere. The power company disconnected the electricity and installed a **generator**, but the unexplained events continued to happen.

Anne-Marie Scarbel may have been the cause of the poltergeist in Rosenheim.

Paranormal researchers were called in. They noticed that the incidents only happened when a young employee, Anne-Marie Scarbel, was in the office. She was not happy at work and disliked her employer. She said events like this had happened in other places she had worked. When she left the office in 1968, the disturbances stopped.

Researchers say young people like Anne-Marie Scarbel are a **common factor** in poltergeist events. They are at the center of the disturbances. The majority of poltergeist events have been connected to unhappy young people. One idea is that poltergeists come into being because these young people have extra emotional energy that they cannot express another way.

Do You Believe in Poltergeists?

There is no question that unexplained disturbances have happened. But are they the work of poltergeists? Could such things really exist? Or are these events just tricks being played by young people? If they are not tricks, is it possible the emotions of young people are somehow causing the appearance of poltergeists?

Researchers continue to collect the evidence, but no one can know for sure if poltergeists are **mischievous** spirits or simply mischievous people.

Glossary

arson: the criminal act of purposefully setting fire to property

amplify: to increase the volume of a sound or sounds

common factor: something that is the same in different sets of circumstances or events

diptheria: a highly contagious infection that causes a sore throat, fever, and coughing

exorcize: to attempt to drive an evil spirit out of a person or a place

fluorescent light tubes: lamps in the form of tubes in which bright electric light is produced

generator: a machine that changes mechanical energy into electrical energy

hoax: a trick done to deceive people, either for fun or to harm

mischievous: describes naughty behavior intended to cause minor harm or trouble

mongoose: a rodent-like mammal found in Africa and Asia

paranormal: events that cannot be explained by science

Protestantism: the second largest form of Christianity. It started in the sixteenth century as an alternative to the Roman Catholic Church.

seizures: sudden abnormal electrical pulses in the brain that cause physical muscle spasms or unconsciousness

telekinesis: the ability to move objects using only a person's mind

Further Information

About Poltergeists
https://psychicscience.org/polt1.aspx

Johnson, C. M. *Hauntings*. Fremont, CA: Full Tilt Press, 2018.

Kovacs, Vic. *Haunted Towns and Villages*. New York: Crabtree Publishing Company, 2018.

Seeley, M H. *Freaky Stories About the Paranormal*. New York: Gareth Stevens Publishing, 2016.

Signs and Stages of Poltergeist Activity
https://weird-world.net/2015/06/07/signs-and-stages-of-poltergeist-activity/

The Story of Gef
http://gefmongoose.blogspot.com/p/the-story-of-gef.html

What is a Poltergeist?
https://www.thoughtco.com/what-is-a-poltergeist-2594093

What Makes a House Feel Haunted?
https://www.psychologytoday.com/us/blog/out-the-ooze/201511/what-makes-house-feel-haunted

Wood, Alix. *Haunted Houses*. New York: Gareth Stevens Publishing, 2017.

Index

Photo Acknowledgments

The images in this book are used with the permission of: ©Shutterstock/donates, p. 1; ©Shutterstock/Clive Watkins, p. 4-5; ©iStockphoto.com/Davy3 Photo, p. 6-7; ©iStockphoto.com/AVTG, p. 8; © Shutterstock/photolike, p. 9; ©Shutterstock/Stocksnapper, p. 10; ©iStockphoto.com/mokee81, p. 11; ©Alamy/Chronicle, p. 12-13; © Public Domain, p. 14; ©Public Domain, p. 15; ©iStockphoto.com/JoeDphoto, p. 16; ©iStockphoto.com/Fer Gregorys, p. 17; ©Shutterstock/pum_eva, sa, p. 18-19; ©Topfoto/Fortean, p. 20; ©Shutterstock/Vintage Visuals, p. 21; ©Topfoto/Fortean, p. 22; ©Topfoto/Fortean, p. 23; ©Topfoto/Fortean/Hart-Davis, p. 24-25; ©iStockphoto.com/Bahadir Tannover, p. 26; ©Public Domain, p. 27; ©Topfoto/Charles Walker, p. 28; ©iStockphoto.com/asbe, p. 29.

Front Cover: ©iStockphoto.com/Fer Gregory.

Brown Bear Books has made every attempt to contact the copyright holder. If anyone has any information please contact licensing@brownbear.co.uk